MAURIE FIELDS'

Dinkum Aussie Jokes

MAURIE FIELDS'
Dinkum Aussie Jokes

Val Jellay

Jokes compiled by
Marty Fields

NH
NEW
HOLLAND

Published in Australia in 1997 by
New Holland Publishers Pty Ltd
3/2 Aquatic Drive
Frenchs Forest
NSW 2086 Australia

Typesetter: Midland Typesetters
Printed in Australia by McPhersons Printing Group, Maryborough

National Library of Australia Cataloguing-in-Publication Data

Fields, Maurie.
Maurie fields' dinkum Aussie jokes.

Includes index.
ISBN 1 86436 292 8

1. Australian wit and humour. I. Jellay, Val, 1927– . II. Fields, Marty.
III. Title. IV. Title: Dinkum Aussie jokes

A828.302

PHOTOGRAPHIC ACKNOWLEDGEMENTS

Channel Nine 'The Flying Doctors', p125; Channel Nine 'Ray Martin's Midday Show', p.56 (top); Channel Nine 'Hey Hey It's Saturday', p.124 (top); Fiona Hamilton (David Atkins 'Soft Shoe Shuffle'), p.90; Don Hudson/HSV 7 'Sunnyside Up', p.91 (bottom); Earle Mant/ABC TV 'Bellbird', p.57; David Parker (Melbourne Theatre Company), p.33; Seven Network 'Bobby Dazzler', p.69; George Wallace (Tivoli Circuit), p.45.

Every effort has been made to trace the original source of copyright material contained in this book. The publisher would be pleased to hear from copyright holders to rectify any errors or omissions.

Whenever the name Maurie Fields is mentioned, it is always with a smile. Although Maurie was an all-round master of entertainment, his humour is without question the great legacy left to us all.

With his preference for Australian outback yarns, it is easy to conjure up an image of the man and his rich, resonant delivery of a gag.

Although the human race will always continue to hunger for laughter, Maurie Fields' legion of loyal fans can once again be part of his audience, as this varied collection of favourites remains with us forever.

Val Jellay

Marty and Val, proud recipients of Maurie's posthumous Logie Award.

INTRODUCTION

Jokes! Jokes! Jokes! We all enjoy laughter as though it is as essential to our well-being as breathing. Since the beginning of time, it has always been good to have a joke teller around.

If every doctor was a good joke teller, we could all be cured of many ailments in a shorter time – even doctors acknowledge that laughter is the best medicine! Unfortunately most doctors don't, won't or can't tell jokes.

Just like training to be a doctor, a good, well-told joke can be the outcome of a number of years in perfecting the art of delivery. The telling of jokes can also die a death if not administered with care.

So it's JOKES in large doses that we can't do without. Take your medicine from these pages and enjoy a feeling of well-being as a result.

MAURIE'S WISDOM

There's a real art to joke telling. How many times have we heard someone say with great enthusiasm, 'I heard a funny joke the other day, wish I could remember it.' Then there are those who begin to relate a joke they've heard – only to falter halfway through, forgetting what it was all about but still laughing at the memory.

We are probably all familiar with the amateur joke teller who is determined to hold a listener's interest by making the joke longer, and longer, believing that diversions in the telling will make the ending funnier. Usually all that is achieved is a loss of interest! Listening to a joke being told by a professional comedian, particularly one respected for their humour, puts us in a mood of happy anticipation because we know that it will be worthwhile.

To work, the written joke has to be able to stand on the words alone, unless we can visualise a particular style of humorist while reading the joke. Who better to visualise than the happy, friendly, distinctive joke teller, Maurie Fields, with the familiar voice that commanded every court to laugh at his jesting?

The greatest impact on Maurie's approach to humour was the Australian people themselves – especially the battlers who always smile in the face of adversity. After the pioneers of the outback made their mark long ago, following generations wore the scars of floods, dust storms, bush fires and general heart-breaking havoc. The outward toughness of these people concealed a softness; the seemingly humourless became our precious yarn-spinning characters.

Decades of coping with nature's hazards moulded the folk Maurie Fields enjoyed. It's their tall tales that are the foundation of Aussie jokes.

I used to take me sheila behind a prickly pear bush.
That makes 'em shift about a bit.

*A*n old fella went to the doctor. He told the doc that he felt terrible, that he was scared he might die. The doctor examined him and told him to stop smoking, stop drinking and stop chasing women.

Will that make me live longer? asked the old bloke.

The doctor said: *No, but it will seem longer.*

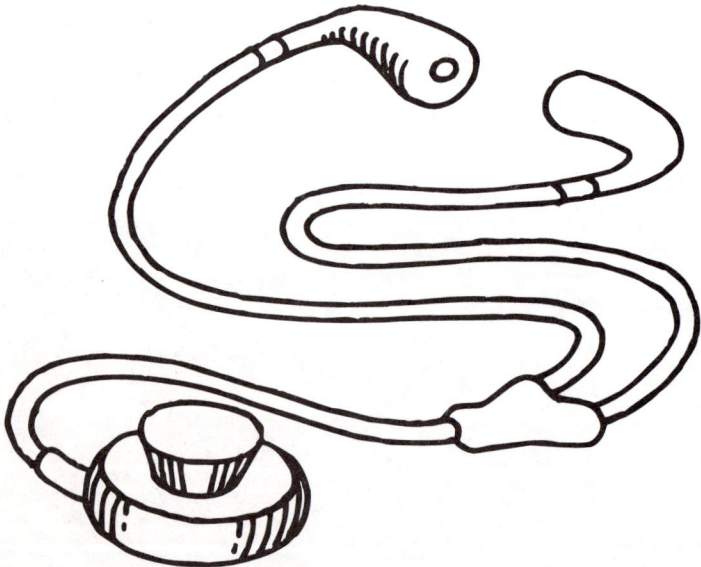

*A*n Aussie went down to the bank to apply for a loan. The people from the bank told him they'd come to his house the next day with their answer to his application.

When he got home that night he said to his son: *Rupert, there's a man coming to see us tomorrow but I want you to tell him I'm not here. I want you to tell him I'm at the office where I make two hundred thousand a year.*

But Dad, said Rupert, *you're unemployed.*

I know that, you idiot, said the Aussie. *I want you to lie. And I also want you to say your mother isn't here. Say she's down at the Art Gallery, selling her paintings for ten thousand each.*

Alright Dad, I'll do it. The bank will be sure to give you the loan, said the boy.

So the next morning there was a knock at the door. Mum and Dad hid in the bedroom, and Rupert went to answer it. There was a man in a suit, with a briefcase, standing there. *Hello*, said the man. *Is your father home?*

No Sir, said the boy, *he's at the office where he earns two hundred thousand a year.*

Is that so? said the man. *How about your mother?*

The boy said: *Sorry, but she's an artist and she's busy at the gallery, selling her paintings for ten grand each.*

Ten grand each, eh? said the man. *Well, would you mind giving them a message for me?*

Not at all Sir, said Rupert.

Lovely, said the man. *When they get home, can you tell them a Taxation Department Inspector dropped by.*

*T*wo drunks were walking down past the Newmarket Sales Yards at midnight, when a dirty great big steer jumped over the fence.

One of the blokes grabbed the steer by the horns, wrestled it all over the road and finally threw it back over the fence.

He turned to his mate and said: *Hey, did you see me fix that bloody lair on the bike?*

A bloke was driving through Victoria when his car began to overheat, so he pulled up at the next farm he saw. The farmer was sitting on the front verandah with a three-legged pig beside him.

G'day, said the bloke. *Car's runnin' hot. Mind if I grab some water?*

Help yourself, said the farmer.

So the bloke pulled the bonnet up and waited for the car to cool down.

That's a nice pig you've got there, said the bloke.

He's better than nice, said the farmer, *he's a bloody miracle.*

That so? said the bloke.

This is an amazing pig, said the farmer. *One time, the barn caught fire, and this pig woke all the other animals and herded them out to safety. Another day, my daughter was swimming in the dam and got into trouble, so the pig jumped in the water and dragged her out.*

Remarkable, said the bloke.

And a further testament to the amazingness of this pig, said the farmer, *was when I was working the back paddock with the tractor, and as I was walking down the hill, the brake on the tractor slipped and it started rolling toward me. It would have crushed me, had the pig, this pig, not jumped into the tractor's cabin and turned the steering wheel so it missed me.*

Extraordinary, said the bloke, *but tell me, how come he's only got three legs?*

The farmer said: *Well, a pig that good, you don't eat all at once.*

A man came home and called to his wife: *Darling, I'm home, and I've got myself that new hearing aid. It's amazing. It's smaller than a fingernail, flesh-toned, stereo, solar-powered, and is designed to fit individually into a single ear. It's just marvellous!*

His wife came into the room saying: *It sounds tremendous, George. How much was it?*

The man said: *It's half past four.*

A Jewish man rang the newspaper to place a death notice about his wife who'd passed away overnight. After he was connected to the obituaries section, the operator told him to go ahead.

Wife Dead, he said.

Is that it? asked the operator.

Yep, two words, Wife Dead, bill me, said the Jewish bloke.

The operator said: *We can't bill you for two words, Sir. We have a one-line minimum. That's five words.*

I'm not paying for five words, I'm paying for two words. Wife Dead. Bill me! said the Jewish bloke.

The operator said: *I'm sorry Sir, but it's company policy. One line, five-word minimum charge. Look, you can have your two words, but you've got three words left over: it's up to you whether you use them or not. But you'll be paying for them.*

There was a pause then the Jewish bloke said: *Alright, alright! Wife Dead. Volvo For Sale.*

*M*oses was on top of a mountain minding his own business, when a booming voice from the heavens spoke to him.

Moses, said the voice, *Moses, this is God.*

Really? said Moses.

Yes, said God, *really. Moses, I have something for you. Take these commandments, Moses.*

Commandments? said Moses, *I don't need any commandments.*

God said: *You must take these commandments, Moses.*

Moses said: *Thanks, but I really don't want them.*

Take the commandments! said God.

Will you stop with the commandments. I don't want them, said Moses.

God was outraged. *Moses, if you don't take these commandments a blackness will fall over the world and humanity will be doomed for eternity!*

Moses said: *Alright, enough with the guilt trip. I'll take some commandments, if it'll make you happy. How much are they?*

God said: *What do you mean, how much are they? They're free!*

Really? said Moses. *I'll take ten!*

*A*n Irish bloke was walking down the road near Dublin, carrying a sack over his shoulder, when he ran into his mate.

Hello Paddy.

Hello Mick. What's in the sack?

Chickens, said the bloke.

How many chickens? asked his mate.

If you can guess, I'll give you the both of them, said the bloke.

His mate said: *Three?*

*A*n Aussie and an American were fishing together on a lake. In the boat with them were their two dogs.

The Aussie said to the Yank: *My dog's amazing. He can do anything.*

So can mine, said the Yank.

Oh yeah? Well watch this, said the Aussie.

He whispered in his dog's ear and it quickly jumped overboard into the lake, swam to shore, ran up the bank to the Aussie's car, jumped in through the window, opened the esky, got a can of beer in its mouth, jumped back out the window, ran down to the lake, swam back out to the boat and, without losing the beer, scrambled back into the dinghy and dropped the beer at the Aussie's feet.

Not bad, said the Yank. *Now have a look at my dog.*

He whispered in his dog's ear and the Yank's dog jumped overboard but, instead of going into the water, the dog walked across the top of the lake, not even getting wet. It reached the bank, up to the car, in the window, got another beer, back down to the lake, and walked back out across the surface of the water, jumped into the boat, and placed the beer at the Yank's feet.

Did you notice anything different? asked the Yank.

Sure did, said the Aussie, *your dog can't swim.*

*T*wo Australian tourists were on holiday in Asia when some monkeys stole their traveller's cheques.

They ran up to their tour guide, yelling: *Mr Wong, Mr Wong, some monkeys stole our traveller's cheques.*

The tour guide said: *Oh no, what kind were they?*

The tourists said: *Brown ones with red bums!!*

So I said to 'er, I said – Go and shake ya hair and give the fowls a feed.

With Mustard – Garlic – and Red Pepper!!!

I only drink when I smoke. I'm down to eight cartons a day.

*A*n old woman went to her doctor.

Doc, she said, *I want a hysterectomy.*

The doctor was amazed. *But Betty,* he said. *You're eighty-three years old. Why do you want a hysterectomy?*

Because, she said, *I've got sixteen grandchildren and that's enough!*

*B*ill walked up to his mate, Frank, at the pub one night.

Frank, he said, *do you want to play golf with John and me tomorrow?*

Frank said: *No thanks mate. It looks like rain. But you blokes go. You know, it's amazing how much golf you two play. I reckon you've played together every day for the last five years.*

Bill said: *Well, we do love our golf. Alright then, I'll see you tomorrow night.* And then he left.

The next night he walked into the pub, looking a bit depressed. Frank was there and asked him if he'd had a bad day.

The worst, said Bill. *First of all, it was pouring. I forgot my jacket. John birdied the first hole, and I scored four over.*

That's awful, said Frank.

That's not the worst of it, said Bill, *on the second green, John had a heart attack and died!*

Frank said: *My God. That's terrible!*

You're telling me! Bill said. *Imagine the rest of my day. Hit the ball, drag John, hit the ball, drag John.*

A woman was in her backyard, when she heard her neighbour's kid crying. She stuck her head over the side fence and asked the little girl what was wrong.

My doggie's old and I'm scared that he's going to die, and I've had him since I was a baby, said the kid.

Well, don't cry, she said, *if he does die, you'll bury him underneath that pretty tree, you'll say a prayer, then Mummy and Daddy will prepare a wake for him, which is when all your friends will come over and bring you presents and there'll be cake and lemonade and lollies.*

The little girl said: *Can we kill him now?*

A woman was in the shower, washing her hair when she heard her doorbell ring.

Who is it? she called.

It's alright M'am, I'm only a blind man, came the response.

Damn charities, she thought, and hopped out of the shower. She couldn't find a towel, but she thought: *How much can a blind man see?* After grabbing two dollars from her purse, she opened her door, naked, and invited him inside.

The man said: *Where do you want your blinds?*

*T*wo coppers from the search and rescue squad were hunting an escaped prisoner in the bush, when one of them spotted some tracks.

Hey Sarge, he said, *what do you reckon these are? They look like dog tracks to me.*

The Sergeant had a look. *No, Senior Constable*, he said, *those are rabbit tracks.*

I think they're dog tracks, said the Constable.

They're rabbit tracks! said the Sergeant.

Dog tracks! said the Constable.

Rabbit tracks! said the Sergeant.

And while they were arguing a train ran over the both of them.

*A*n old Jewish man was on his deathbed. Around him, his family had come to pay their final respects.

He opened his eyes in the dimly lit room, and moaned: *Rachel, my faithful wife, Rachel, are you here with me?*

Yes, Hymie, she said, *I'm here with you.*

He said: *Jacob, my eldest son, are you here with me now?*

Jacob said: *Yes, Poppa, I'm here.*

And Michael, continued the man, *Michael, my youngest boy, are you here for me now?*

Yes Poppa, said Michael, *I'm here with you.*

Hymie said: *And my only daughter, my beautiful princess, Bettina, are you here with me?*

His daughter, weeping, said: *Yes, Poppa, I'm here; we're all here.*

All of you? said Hymie. *So who's minding the shop?*

A bloke went into a restaurant. After looking at the exclusive menu, he called the manager over and asked if he could get plain old steak and eggs. The manager said he would see what he could do.

Wait a minute, said the bloke, *don't I know you?*

I'm not sure, said the manager, *your face looks familiar too.*

You're Franky Johnstone, aren't you? said the bloke. *We went to school together 20 years ago. Wanky Franky, we used to call you.*

Ah yes, said the manager, *Herbert Smith, how could I forget. And how are you?*

I'm alright, said Herb. *Jeez, you look like you're doing alright.*

Yes, said Frank, *I own this place. And my wife is the chef. Also I play the cello in the Symphony Orchestra, while my wife plays the flute. We have two children. My son is a master of the violin, and my daughter plays piano. You must bring your family over to our house one evening and we'll give you a recital.*

Well, that'd be lovely, said the bloke. *I work as a bouncer now, after retiring from the ring. My wife's a lady wrestler. My son's just got out after doing two years for assault, and my daughter learns karate. You should bring your family over to our joint and we'll give you a bloody good hiding!*

A bloke working in a factory chopped all his fingers off in a machine. He rushed to the hospital in a panic.

The surgeon said: *Now calm down Sir. These days, with microsurgery, we can easily join your fingers back on. Now where are the fingers?*

I haven't got them, said the bloke.

The surgeon said: *But why not?*

The bloke said: *I couldn't pick them up!*

*C*orporal Brown was based at Puckapunyal Army Base. While he was doing his time there, his father died. The news came to him via his Drill Sergeant.

The Drill Sergeant lined the squad up at attention in front of their barracks and shouted: *Corporal Brown, step forward.*

Brown stepped forward. *Brown,* said the Sergeant, *your father's dropped dead!*

The Corporal was devastated and collapsed to the ground, crying and howling. When the Company Commander heard how brutally the news had been delivered to Corporal Brown, he hauled the Sergeant up to his office. *Sergeant,* he said, *that was the most insensitive piece of work I've ever heard of. How could you be so hard on the boy? Don't be so straightforward next time. Show some inventiveness when delivering that sort of news!*

Yes Sir. Sorry Sir, said the Sergeant.

About a month later, news came that poor old Corporal Brown's mother had passed away. So, the Sergeant lined up the squad in front of the barracks again. *Company, attention! Now, all soldiers whose mothers are still alive, take one step forward . . . where do you think you're going, Brown?*

*T*wo old school friends ran into each other at a pub. They'd been very close at school, so were delighted to see each other.

Well if it isn't Dave Johnson, said one, *how've you been?*

Well, hello Bert, said Dave, *I've been very well, thanks. And what about you and your family. How's your Dad?*

Bert said: *Not good. He got hit by a train and killed.*

Dave said: *Oh gawd, that's awful. How's your Mum?*

Well, said Bert, *the shock of Dad's death gave her a heart attack, and she died too.*

That's terrible, said Dave, *How's your brother, Peter?*

Pete's doing fifteen years for murder, said Bert

Your sister, Doreen? asked Dave.

She's got three kids to a bloke and he won't marry her. Mind you, said Bert, *I'm going alright. I've got a job selling lucky charms.*

MAURIE'S WISDOM

Australians identify with a good Aussie yarn, especially if it means, in effect, laughing at themselves. Their ability to seemingly take life's setbacks in their stride even spills over into their distinctive laid-back style of speech and turn-of-phrase.

Many factors have influenced the Aussie accent over the years, just as colloquial expressions adopted by Australians have their roots in many cultures. The gloriously laconic accent of a dinkum Aussie, epitomised by the resonance of our own Maurie Fields, has been passed down from generation to generation.

One particularly humorous idiom that has made its mark on Australians in more ways than one is the rhyming slang of cockney London. From our early colonial days, this parlance has appealed to the Australian sense of humour. Even today, rhyming slang is still popular with those who wish to include a touch of humour in their everyday conversation.

'Going for a pickle and pork (walk), up the frog and toad (road)' is just one example of the many quirky phrases commonly heard in cockney London. Such phrases soon made their way into the Aussie vernacular, and it wasn't long before the local wags adopted rhyming slang and localised it, perhaps forgetting its origins along the way.

It takes a real expert, though, to string together effective dinkum Aussie rhyming slang such as:

You should see the Dutch pegs (legs) on my Charlie Wheeler (sheila). I bought her some tippy canoes (shoes); we caught a bread and jam (tram) and went to the chocolate mixtures (pictures). She whacked me across the north and south (mouth) with her tit for tat (hat) just because I put my German band (hand) through her Warwick Farm (arm). Just as well I didn't go for the Violet Crumble (fumble)!

People still enjoy rhyming slang today. It suits the Aussie personality perfectly. It is colourful and can purposely exclude an otherwise knowledgeable linguist.

Nice drink. It's a cross between Muscatel and Hock, I call it Muck.

*A*n old bloke went to the doctor for a check-up. After examining him, the doctor said, *Percy, I've got two pieces of bad news for you. First, you've got hepatitis.*

The old bloke was horrified. *Oh no, not hepatitis,* he said, *that's terrible. Not hepatitis, anything but hepatitis. Gawd Doc, don't tell me I've got hepatitis.*

The doctor said: *I'm afraid that's not all. You also have Alzheimer's disease.*

Again, the old fella was mortified. *Not Alzheimer's. Anything but Alzheimer's. Don't tell me I've got Alzheimer's. That's absolutely terrible. Oh well, at least I don't have hepatitis.*

A Pom was at Tullamarine airport waiting to get on a plane, when he saw an Aussie sitting on a big trunk. He was looking at his wristwatch and laughing. Feeling curious, he approached the man to ask him what he was laughing at.

Excuse me, said the Pom, *but would you mind telling me what is so funny?*

The Aussie looked up and said: *This video I'm looking at, on my watch.*

The Pom was amazed. *Are you telling me that your watch plays videos?*

Oh sure, said the Aussie, *you can get special miniature-sized cassettes for it. But that's not all it does. It also gets normal TV and SBS, has an electronic compass and it has a tiny pop-up toaster in the side here. As well as that, it's a mobile 'phone, a fax, a computer, and if you flip up the top, a tiny microwave oven. In summer it has a cooling fan, and in winter it's a heater. It also has a searchlight, an alarm and a cigarette lighter!*

The Englishman couldn't believe it. *I simply have to get one of those.*

They only have 'em in Japan, said the Aussie, *but I could let you have this one here, for say, two hundred dollars.*

Two hundred dollars! That's fantastic. I'll take it.

He gave the money to the Aussie, who stood up, handed him the watch, and walked off towards the exit.

The man called after him: *Excuse me, but you've forgotten your trunk.*

No, that's yours too, said the Aussie. *That's the battery.*

*A*n Irish bloke was digging holes of varying sizes in his backyard. His neighbour asked him what he was doing.

I'm digging a hole to bury my dog, said the Irishman.

The neighbour said: *But why have you dug so many holes?*

The Irishman said: *The others were all too small.*

*T*wo American blokes wanted to race a horse in the Kentucky Derby, so they rang their brother who lived in Victoria, Australia. They told him they were sending some money for him to buy an Australian racehorse to send back to America, because everyone knows Aussie horses are the best.

So the bloke in Australia scouted around until he found a lovely three-year-old colt. He took the horse down to the docks, put him in a container and shipped him to America.

Unfortunately the ship stopped in Perth and there was a wharfie's strike, so the horse was off-loaded, sat on the dock for six weeks and, sadly, died. The Perth port authorities rang the bloke in Victoria to tell him the horse was dead.

Send it anyway, said the bloke, so the container was put back on board and sent to America. *It's not my fault*, thought the bloke. *I'll say it died mid-voyage.*

Well, he didn't hear from his brothers for about a year, so he thought he'd better give them a call. He finally got onto them. *How's the horse?* he asked.

We made two million dollars out of him, said his brothers.

The bloke was amazed. *How did you do that? He was dead!*

Oh, we know, they said. *We held a lottery. Two dollars a ticket, and the first prize was an Australian racehorse. We sold a million tickets.*

Didn't anyone complain that the horse was dead? asked the bloke.

Only the fella who won, so we gave him his money back!

*N*orm and Jim went down to the local Catholic church. Jim waited outside while Norm went into the confessional box. *Bless me Father*, he said, *for I have sinned.*

The priest said: *What have you done, my son?*

Norm said: *I've committed adultery, Father.*

Who with? asked the priest.

I can't say, said Norm, *but she's a member of the parish.*

Well, said the priest, *was it that Mrs Johnston down at the bowls club?*

No Father, it wasn't her, said Norm.

Well was it the Miller widow? asked the priest.

No Father, said Norm, *it wasn't her either.*

Alright, said the priest, *your punishment shall be nine Hail Marys and four Our Fathers.*

Thank you Father, said Norm, and left the confessional box. When he got outside, Jim was there waiting for him.

How'd you go? asked Jim.

Not bad, said Norm. *I got nine Hail Marys, four Our Fathers, and a couple of very good leads.*

A visiting cowboy rode into town, tied his white horse up outside the saloon, and walked inside the bar, whistling a happy tune. He stood at the bar in his pale blue cowboy pants and white leather vest and asked for a Fluffy Duck in a balloon glass.

When he finished his drink, he picked up a pale-lemon hanky and carefully removed some froth from his top lip, turned around and walked out through the swinging doors. He was aghast to find that someone had painted his horse *pink*. Furious, he burst back into the saloon.

Who, he yelled, *amongst you here, painted my horse pink?*

A big, butch brute of a bloke with no teeth stepped forward and growled: *I painted your bloody horse pink. What about it?*

The visitor said: *Well, I've just come to tell you: it's ready for the second coat.*

A bloke who'd been arrested was sitting in a Sydney police station waiting to be charged, when a young constable walked in and approached the counter.

Um, Sarge, said the Constable. *Um, we've just been given a report of a dead buffalo that's been hit by a truck, lying in the middle of Quatta Quaneska Lane.*

Well, write up a report, Constable, said the Desk Sergeant.

So the Constable sat on the bench next to the bloke, got out his clipboard and a pen, and began filling in a report form.

'Found', he wrote, *'one buffalo, dead, in brackets, lying in Quatta Quaneska Lane.' That's Q U A T E ... No, Q A T T ... No, Q U A D D E ... No that's not right either. Hey Sarge*, he continued ... *How do you spell 'Quatta Quaneska'?*

The Sergeant said: *You're a copper, aren't you? Find out yourself!*

So the Constable sat for a while, then put down the clipboard and pen and walked out the door. He was back in about half an hour, covered in blood, dirt, manure and sweat.

Gawd, said the bloke, who'd been sitting there all along. *What have you been doing?*

Well, said the young policeman, *I've been dragging a dirty big dead buffalo into Pitt Street.*

A passenger boarded a jumbo jet and asked one of the hostesses to put a parcel in the fridge for him. He explained to her in detail that it was seafood, so she dutifully obliged.

Nearing the end of the long journey, the hostess announced over the public address system: *Would the gentleman who gave me the crabs at the beginning of the flight please come to the rear of the cabin, and I'll give them back to him.*

A big, huge bloke walked into a pub in Dublin. He walked up to a little fella having a drink and said: *Are you Michael O'Shea?*

The little bloke said: *Who wants to know?*

I do, said the big bloke, and grabbed the little fella, punching him in the face. The little bloke just laughed.

The big bloke hit him over the head with a bottle and punched him to the ground. Again, the little bloke laughed.

The big guy jumped up and down on the little fella, and finally smashed a chair over his bruised body. Still the little bloke laughed his head off.

I've beaten you half to death! said the big bloke, *but you won't stop laughing. What's so bloody funny?*

The little bloke still laughing said: *The joke's on you. I'm not Michael O'Shea!*

A drunk was standing on the street in front of a jewellery store that had just been robbed. The coppers arrived and questioned him.

Did you do it? they asked.

No, said the drunk.

Did you see who did it? they asked.

Yes, said the drunk.

Well, who was it? they asked.

He said: *A car pulled up, and an elephant jumped out, smashed the shop window, grabbed the stuff, and took off again.*

The coppers said: *Can you describe the elephant?*

An elephant is an elephant, said the drunk.

On the contrary, said the cops, *Indian elephants have big ears, and African elephants have small ears.*

The drunk said: *I still don't know.*

They said: *Why not?*

He said: *He was wearing a stocking over his head.*

MAURIE'S WISDOM

When silent movies burst open the entertainment scene, they relied heavily on visual humour – the jokes were conveyed to the audience through movement, not sound.

Subtitles were required for an occasional film frame or plot explanation, and the silent movie comedians usually wrote their own storylines, based on a good bit of comedy business.

Hence, comedians who were also acrobats, dancers, jugglers, or even magicians, were valuable, and novel ways of doing prat-falls were in high demand. Slapstick was the order of the day, some of it hair-raisingly dangerous, with the greatest comedy stars all doing their own stunts.

American vaudeville and its predecessor, burlesque, bred generations of very versatile performers. English variety and revue also produced the popular all-round English entertainers.

This melting pot of talent influenced enthusiastic, but geographically isolated Australian humorists at the time, giving them a yardstick by which to create. Australians, however, have long since learnt never to underestimate their home-grown talent, to be proud of their individuality.

We know what is funny and what is not. We have developed our own identity as comedians and no longer have to be reminded that we have our own sense of humour. Aussies can also laugh louder than anyone.

So I said to him, you do the same with ya dog and you can get on the bus.

A bloke took his canary to the vet.

It's not eating, doc, he said.

The vet examined the bird. *His beak's grown too much, so he can't eat. We'll have to file it down.*

How much will that cost? asked the bloke.

About two hundred, but you could do it yourself if you wanted to save the money, said the vet.

For two hundred, I'll do it myself, said the bloke.

Well, be careful, said the vet, *if you file off too much he'll die of beak-shock. And if you don't file off enough, he'll die of beak-rot. Here's a pamphlet showing exactly how the beak should look.*

So the bloke took the bird and the pamphlet home. The next day he was back.

How's the bird? asked the vet.

No bloody good, mate, said the bloke, *he died.*

I told you to be careful! said the vet. *Did you follow the diagram?*

The bloke said: *I filed his beak till it looked exactly like the one in the picture. I was very careful but when I took his head out of the vice, he was DEAD!*

*T*wo racehorses were sitting in a bar, chatting.

It was extraordinary! said one. *Last Saturday at Caulfield, I was coming last by four lengths down the side, with no hope of winning, when a big thunderbolt came out of the sky, hit me between the eyes, and I took off and won by a short half head!*

The other horse said: *Remarkable! The same thing happened to me at Flemington, on Cup Day. I was going backwards in the straight, when a thunderbolt came out of the sky, hit me between the eyes, and I took off and won by a length!*

Just then, a greyhound walked up to the two horses.

Pardon me, he said, *but I couldn't help overhearing your conversation, and the same thing happened to me at Sandown Park, a week ago. I got a bad start and was trailing the field, when a thunderbolt came out of the night sky and hit me between the eyes. I won by six lengths!*

The greyhound walked off, and the first horse said: *Amazing! A talking dog!*

A shark swam up to a squid and said: *Hey Frank, you don't look too good.*

The squid said: *No, Norm, I'm not too well at all.*

So the shark said: *Listen, jump into my mouth and I'll swim you 'round a bit. Then see if you feel better.*

So the squid jumped in the shark's mouth. The shark swam over to a whale and spat the squid at the whale, saying: *Hey Bert, here's the sick squid I owe you.*

A cop car pulled up beside three kids standing in the middle of Pitt Street Mall in Sydney.

C'mere, said the cop.

The boys walked over to the car. The cop said to the first boy: *What's your name?*

The kid didn't want to give his real name so he had a look around him and noticed a department store. *David Jones*, he said.

Very cute, said the copper. He said to the second kid: *What's your name?*

The second kid looked around and said: *George Building Society*.

Bloody smarty, eh? said the copper turning to the third kid. *And what's your name?*

The kid said: *Ken*.

Thank God, said the cop, *that one of you kids has some respect for the law. Now Ken, what's your second name?*

The kid said: *Tucky Fried Chicken!*

A knockabout bloke was down on his luck and couldn't find work, so he caught the bus to Vaucluse, a very ritzy Sydney suburb, to knock on people's front doors, asking for odd jobs. He walked up the driveway to a huge mansion and rang the doorbell.

When a man answered, he asked: *Got any odd jobs need doing?*

Actually, said the gent, *I need my porch painted. It's around the back.*

No worries, said the bloke.

So the man gave him a 10-litre tin of green paving paint and sent the bloke around to paint the back porch. About three hours later, the bloke came round the front and rang the doorbell again.

I've finished, he said. *Nice job too. Two coats.*

Fine, said the gent, *here's twenty bucks.*

Thanks, said the bloke and began to leave.

As he was walking down the driveway he turned and shouted: *By the way, I don't think it was a Porch, it looked more like a Ferrari.*

A school teacher bent down to pick up her chalk and her dress rode up a bit.

Miss, a little boy said with his hand up. *I just saw your lovely knees.*

You naughty little boy, she said. *Go home and don't come back for the rest of the week.*

Then she leant over and another boy said: *Miss, I just saw your cleavage!*

Get out! she said. *And don't come back for a month.*

Then the teacher caught her skirt on a nail and it came off completely. A little boy started packing up his books.

Where are you going? she asked.

He said: *Well, with what I just saw, my school days are over!*

A bloke went to a golf course and entered the pro shop.

I want to hire a caddy with good eyesight because I keep losing my golf balls, said the bloke.

The golf pro said: *We've got a bloke here who's amazing. Eyes like a hawk.*

Fine, said the bloke, *I'll meet him at the first tee.*

When he got there, there was a 92-year-old man standing there waiting for him.

Are you my caddy? asked the bloke. *I asked for someone with good eyes!*

My eyesight is perfect, said the old bloke, *I have the eyes of a ten-year-old. Henry the Hawk, they call me.*

The golfer said: *Alright Henry, keep an eye on this ball. I tend to go off-track a bit.*

He hit the ball, a wild hook, and it finished somewhere out to the left. He turned to the caddy. *Henry*, he said, *did you see it?*

Yes, Sir, said Henry.

Well, where is it? asked the bloke.

Henry said: *I forget.*

*T*wo snakes were sitting in the bush.

One of the snakes said: *Hey Stan, are we poisonous?*

Oh, God yes, said the second snake.

That's no good, said the first snake.

Why's that? said the second.

The first snake said: *'Cause I just bit my tongue!*

A bloke went into prison and was put in with the long-termers. On his first day, his cell mate took him around the jail, introducing him to the other long-term prisoners. First, he took him into the laundry.

Hey boys, he said, *this here's George. He's gonna be with us for a while. And by the way fellas, twenty-three.*

The men in the laundry burst into hysterical laughter. George was puzzled. Next, he was taken into the woodwork room.

Hey fellas, said his cell mate, *this here's George. And by the way boys, nine.* The men just about exploded with laughter. George was very confused.

What's with the number thing? Why do those blokes laugh when you say a number? he asked.

Well, it's like this, said his cell mate. *We've all been in here together for a very long time, so we all know the same jokes. So rather than tell the whole joke, we've numbered them. You just say the number, and we know what joke it stands for, and we laugh.*

I see, said George. *Listen mate,* he said. *You could do me a favour. I want to make a good impression here, so tell me, what's a sure-fire gag?*

Number seventeen, said his cell mate, *it's a classic. Never fails.*

Great, said George, *number seventeen, thanks.*

His cell mate led him into the dining hall. *Hey fellas,* he said, *this is George.*

G'day, said George. *Good to meet you. And by the way, seventeen.* Nobody laughed. *I said, 'seventeen',* said George. Again, not a soul laughed. Not even a chuckle.

Thanks a lot! George said to his cell mate as they left. *They didn't even smile!*

I can't understand it, said his cell mate, *it must have been the way you told it.*

A drunk was in a pub and wanted to go to the toilet. He asked the barmaid how to find it.

She said: *First on the right, first on the left and you can't miss it.*

So he took the first on the right, and then took the first on the right again. It was a lift well, he fell in, and landed *WHOOSH* at the bottom.

Looking up, he screamed: *DON'T FLUSH IT! DON'T FLUSH IT!!*

I was playing me ukulele during the big flood, and floated straight out the window. Marty accompanied me on the piano.

I ordered a beer and a wine for me mate. The barman said 'Red or white?' I said 'It doesn't matter, he's bloody colour blind!'

I can read writing, and I can write reading, but this writin' is written rotten.

*A*n old bloke was a keen golfer but he was terribly bad at it. One day, he went out to his favourite course to have a round by himself and, as he teed up for the first, God spoke to him.

Frank Johnston, said God, *Frank, this is your lucky day!*

Frank was amazed. He hit off from the first, bounced off a tree, hit a power line, and landed on the green, an inch from the hole.

Gawd, said Frank. He birdied the hole. On the next, he hit off, and the ball struck a car in the carpark, bounced off the bonnet and landed in the hole!

This is unbelievable, said Frank. He was having the most amazing day of his life. His luck was extraordinary.

He arrived at the last hole, four under the card. The final hole required players to hit over a huge gorge. Frank had never made the distance before, so he went to his bag and got out an old ball.

Frank, said God, *put down a new ball.*

But God, said Frank.

Don't 'but God' me! said God. *Take away the old ball. Put down a new one.*

So Frank teed up a new ball.

Now, said God, *have a practice swing.*

So Frank had a practice swing.

There was a pause, then God said: *Put back the old ball.*

*F*our kids in the country were riding on a horse down the side of the road. A cityslicker came driving by in his Saab. Seeing the unusual sight of four kids on one horse, he decided to have a bit of fun. He pulled up beside them and said: *Hey kids, got room for one more?*

The kid sitting at the back of the horse turned around, lifted the horse's tail, and said: *Yeah, you can hop in the boot if you like!*

A Jewish bloke was skiing up in the Swiss Alps when he was accidentally buried under an avalanche of snow. The Red Cross sent out a search party. For days they searched frantically and after finding the man's skis they began to dig down to him. *Mr Goldstein*, they yelled to him, *Mr Goldstein! It's the Red Cross.*

A faint voice from deep down under the snow yelled: *I gave already.*

*A*n Aussie bought a house in the middle of the Nevada Desert in America. On his first day, when he was sitting on his verandah, he saw a cloud of dust on the horizon. It turned out to be a Yank on a motorbike.

The American pulled up at the house and called out: *Howdy, neighbour!*

Neighbour? questioned the Aussie. *We're in the middle of a desert!*

Yep, said the Yank, *I'm your closest neighbour. I live eighty-five miles down the road. I've come to welcome you to the neighbourhood and let you know that there's a 'Welcome To The Neighbourhood' party in your honour at my house tonight. Oh, you've gotta come. There'll be drinks, music, food and afterwards we'll have a wild sex orgy!*

The Aussie said: *Beauty! I'm coming. What should I wear?*

Oh, that don't matter, said the Yank, *there'll only be the two of us.*

A boy took his essay on the family dog up to his English teacher for marking.

When she'd read it, she said: *Billy, two years ago, I asked your brother Simon to write an essay on the family dog. This is exactly the same essay. How do you explain that?*

Billy said: *Of course it's the same essay. It's the same dog.*

*A*n Italian immigrant, Gino, arrived on a ship at Station Pier, Port Melbourne, looking for a new start in a new country. His brother had come out about ten years before and had joined the fire brigade. When he met up with his brother, the first thing that impressed Gino was the uniform.

That's a beautiful uniform youra wearing, said Gino. *All I want is a job where I can wear a beautiful uniform too.*

So off he went to look for work. The first place he tried was the Kraft Cheese factory. They offered him a job on the production line.

Does it come with a uniform? asked Gino.

Well, you get this nice blue dustcoat, said the bloke from the factory.

Ok, I'll take it. Gino couldn't wait to tell his brother about his new job at Kraft and show him his new uniform.

That Friday night, they arranged to meet at a local pub. While Gino was waiting for his brother to arrive, a Salvation Army officer came through the bar, selling the 'War Cry' and asking for donations.

Gino stopped him and said: *'scusa me, Sir, but that is the most wonderful uniform I ever seen! Who do you work for?*

The Salvo said: *Why, I work for the Lord Jesus.*

What a coincidence! said Gino. *I work for his brother, Kraft Cheeses!*

*J*eff Kennett, the Premier of Victoria, Bob Carr, the Premier of New South Wales, and John Howard, the Prime Minister, were travelling in a car on their way back from a political conference in the country when they got a flat tyre. They had no spare, so had to walk to a farmhouse. They knocked on the door and when the farmer answered, they asked if they could stay the night. The farmer said he only had two spare beds, so one of the politicians would have to sleep in the barn.

Bob Carr said: *I don't mind roughing it. I'll sleep out there.*

So they all went to bed. At about midnight, there was a knock at the door. It was Bob Carr in his pyjamas.

Listen, he said. *I can't stay in the barn. There's a cow and a pig in there and I can't stand cows. It's an allergy.*

Jeff Kennett said: *Alright, I'll sleep in the barn.*

So again they all went to bed. At about 2.00 a.m. there was a knock at the door. It was Jeff.

I'm sorry, he said. *I'd love to sleep out there with the cow and pig, but I'm allergic to hay.*

So John Howard stepped forward: *I'll sleep in the bloody barn!*

So once more, they all went to bed. About a half an hour later, there was a knock at the door. It was the cow and the pig.

*A*n Irishman walked up to the SP Bookie in a pub.

I'll have twenty dollars on 'Moonshine' in the Cup, he said.

Right, you're on, said the bookie.

The race was live on TV and they watched Moonshine run last.

I'll have another twenty dollars on 'Moonshine', said the Irishman, later that night.

Right, you're on, said the bookie.

Of course, Moonshine ran last. When the Irishman came to pay up, the bookie couldn't help asking: *Paddy, you saw Moonshine get beaten this afternoon. Why d'you back him tonight?*

The Irishman said: *I thought he might have needed the run!*

*I*n the Old West, the Sheriff walked into the local saloon.

I'm looking, he said, *for the Brown Paper Cowboy.*

One of the locals asked: *Well, what's he look like, Sheriff?*

The Sheriff said: *Well, he's got a brown paper hat, brown paper shirt, brown paper trousers, he rides a brown paper horse, he's got a brown paper gun, and it fires brown paper bullets!*

The locals asked: *What's he wanted for?*

Rustling, said the Sheriff.

A keen golfer was in a seaside town and went to the local golf course for a round. He was looking for a partner and was directed to a local fellow sitting beside the first tee, which was positioned at the edge of a huge ravine overlooking the ocean. To land on the green you had to hit over the water.

G'day! said the bloke, *Fancy a round?*

Sure, said the local, *I've been playing this course for twenty-five years*.

They tossed a coin and the local was to hit off first. He went to his bag, got out a new ball, took it out of its box, put it on the tee, swung and hit it straight into the water.

Bad luck, said the bloke. *Have another go.*

So the local went to his bag, got out another new ball, took it out of its box, put it on the tee, swung, and again, hit it into the ocean.

Not again! said the bloke. *Have another go.*

So the local went to his bag, got out a new ball, took it out of its box, put it on the tee, but before he could hit it, the bloke said: *Mate, you keep hitting 'em into the water. Why don't you use an old ball?*

The local said: *I've never had one!*

MAURIE'S WISDOM

Partnerships in joke telling have surely been around since the first joke was ever told. Today's audiences are familiar with the names of past double acts such as Abbott and Costello, George Burns and Gracie Allen and Martin and Lewis, whose fame reached Australia by way of the movies. Most of their successful movies were written around comedy routines that had been polished and perfected over many years of performing in front of live audiences in hundreds of venues, including the popular vaudeville and variety theatres.

Each partner in a successful double act is responsible for a joke and getting a laugh. If a joke isn't set up properly with the key words stressed in the right place, the comedian has nothing to bounce off. That's why the 'straight man' is called a 'feed'. He 'feeds' the straight lines to the comedian. Bud Abbott of Abbott and Costello was a renowned straight man. He pulled and pushed Lou Costello into physical as well as verbal situations, and most of the time no-one noticed. That's the art of concealing the art.

With the exposure of joke tellers and comedy double acts in the world of television, one performance can reach millions in a matter of minutes. The constant turnover of comedy routines can become a nightmare. New ideas, new approaches and new jokes have to be constantly created. The likes of Morecombe and Wise, Peter Cook and Dudley Moore, Hale and Pace, the Two Ronnies, and so on, all successfully transferred their live theatre experience to television.

Farnham and Fields: two loose pages from the Book of Fun.

*T*he West Indies were playing Australia at the MCG at the end of a very bad summer tour.

The 'phone rang in the Windies' dressing room. *This is Mrs Brian Lara calling from Jamaica. Would I be able to speak to my husband?*

The bloke who answered said: *I'm sorry but you've just missed him. He's just gone in to bat.*

She said: *That's fine. I'll hold.*

*T*wo old blokes were on a tractor. They drove it across the paddock, and, without looking for traffic, continued straight out onto the highway.

A young man in a Porsche was doing about 200km on the clock. He came flying around the bend, saw the tractor, swerved left to miss it, crashed through a paddock fence, did a huge circle in the paddock, smashed back through the fence up the other end, back out onto the highway and kept tearing off down the road.

One of the old blokes on the tractor turned to the other and said: *Jeez, Bert, we only just got out of that paddock in time!*

A bloke was out on the town and walked up to a nightclub door, but the bouncer wouldn't let him in.

You don't have a tie on, said the bouncer.

I'll fix this mongrel, thought the bloke, and went back to his car. He opened the boot, got out the jumper leads and tied them around his neck. Then he went back up to the door of the nightclub.

The bouncer saw him and said: *Very good, jumper leads. Alright, you can come in, but don't start anything!*

A motorbike rider saw a hitchhiker standing on the side of the road. It was raining and very cold and the bloke was dressed only in a singlet and a pair of shorts. The rider took pity on him and gave him a lift.

When they got going, the passenger was freezing so the bike rider gave him a spare leather jacket to wear and said: *The zip's broken, it won't do up, but if you wear it back to front, it'll keep you warm.*

He also gave him a full face helmet so the passenger was as snug as a bug in a rug. About 10km down the road, the rider turned round and noticed his passenger had fallen off the bike, he did a quick U-turn and went back to search for him.

Five minutes up the road, he found him lying on the ground surrounded by a group of people. He ran up to the bloke.

How is he? he asked.

A woman standing there answered: *He was alright till they tried to turn his head around the right way.*

*T*his fella, his wife and his mother-in-law were up near Darwin on holidays when the mother-in-law went missing. The bloke waited a couple of days then called the coppers.

When did you last see her? asked the police.

The last time I saw her, said the bloke, *she was walking down to the mangrove swamp.*

The police conducted a search and rang the bloke at about four o'clock in the morning.

We've located your mother-in-law, they said. *Sadly, she's lying face down in the mangrove swamp, with two of the biggest mud crabs you've ever seen sitting on her back. What do you want us to do?*

The bloke said: *Well, you take one, send me the other one and then reset the bait.*

*A*t a huge supernatural convention, a speaker addressed the large crowd.

Now as we know, he said, *ghosts exist. I'd like to conduct an experiment. Would all the people who've seen a ghost raise their hands.*

About half the crowd raised their hands.

Alright, he said, *now keep your hand raised if you've actually spoken to a ghost.*

About a quarter of the crowd had their hands up.

Now, he said, *keep your hand raised if you've actually had some physical contact with a ghost.*

About ten hands were still raised.

Amazing! he said. *Alright, let's try something. Has anybody ever made love to a ghost?*

All hands dropped, except one. A bloke at the back still had his hand raised. The speaker was astounded.

Sir, he said, *you've actually made love to a ghost? Please come up here on stage. Now Sir,* said the speaker, *can you tell us all what it was like to make love to a ghost?*

Ghost? said the bloke, *I thought you said GOAT!*

*A*n Irish bloke in the Irish Paratroopers was being sent on a secret mission.

His captain said: *Alright Murphy, here's the plan. At nine hundred hours, you'll catch the plane at Dublin airport. It'll take you over Germany. At ten thousand feet you'll jump. You parachute down into the valley. There'll be a motorbike there for you. Ride it into the village and shoot the General who's staying there. Is that clear?*

Yes Sir, said Murphy.

So the Irish paratrooper got to the airport, but the nine o'clock plane left at ten o'clock. Then at ten thousand feet he jumped and pulled his chute ripcord. It didn't work. He pulled his emergency chute. Nothing!!

Great, he said, *first the plane was late, now my parachute doesn't work. I bet when I get down there the bloody motorbike won't be there, either!*

A copper pulled a motorist over who was doing about 200km an hour down the middle of a highway.

What do you think you're doing, said the copper, *are you crazy?*

No mate, said the driver.

Well why were you going so fast down the middle of the road? asked the copper.

I'm obeying the instructions on my licence, replied the driver. *See, at the bottom it clearly says: 'Tear along dotted line.'*

A Texan millionaire was a keen golfer so he went to his local priest to ask if there was a golf course in heaven.

I don't know, said the priest. *Try the Bishop, he's higher up than me.*

Thanks Father, said the Texan. He then visited the Bishop.

Father, he said. *Here's a thousand dollars for your church if you can tell me if there's a golf course in heaven.*

I'm not sure, said the Bishop. *Only the Pope would know that sort of thing.*

So the Texan flew to Rome and met with the Pope. *Your holiness*, he said, *here's a million dollars for your church if you can tell me whether there's a golf course in heaven.*

I'm not sure, myself, said the Pope, *I'll get on the 'phone to the Pearly Gates. Wait here.*

The Pope went into his office and picked up the gold 'phone, a direct line to the Pearly Gates. *Peter?* he said. *It's John Paul. How are you? . . . Good. Listen, I've got a man down here, Texan, Ted Thompson, wants to know if there's a golf course in Heaven . . . right . . . ok . . . right, I'll tell him. Thanks.*

The Pope went back out to the Texan. *I've got good news and bad news*, he said.

What's the story? asked the Texan.

Well, the good news, said the Pope, *is yes, there is a golf course in heaven. The bad news is that you tee off at seven o'clock tomorrow morning.*

A woman went to see her doctor.

Doc, she said once she was in his office. *You've got to help me. I've got a terrible flatulence problem – I break wind about once a minute.*

So I hear, said the doctor.

I just can't stop, she said. *It's terribly embarrassing.*

I see, said the doc. *Tell me, how's your diet?*

Normal, she said.

Do you get enough sleep? he asked.

Yes, I do, she said.

Stress? he asked.

No more then usual, she replied.

He sat at his desk writing notes for a moment, then left the office. He was back in a moment with a long, skinny pole with a hook on the end of it.

The woman was terrified. *What are you going to do with that?* she screamed.

The doctor said: *I'm opening a window, it stinks in here.*

MAURIE'S WISDOM

Reflecting on what influenced the Australian sense of humour, it must be said that women have cornered a great share of the joke telling market. Famous early American comediennes were not necessarily tellers of jokes as such, but comedy actresses with incredible timing. They included Lucille Ball, Carole Burnett, Martha Raye, Charlotte Greenwood, Virginia O'Brien, Cass Daley and Betty Hutton. Then there was Hatti Jacques, who headed an equally star-studded line-up of British funny ladies too long to even contemplate.

The main ingredient in a woman's ability to be funny is the way she has been able to exploit her unique characteristics and stereotypical views of how a woman is meant to behave. Even the zany Phyllis Diller, who garnered the majority of her laughs at the expense of her fictitious husband, Fang, had a wardrobe that was over-the-top girlie. The wonderful Lucille Ball could fall flat on her face in a pool of mud and still remain a lady. She played the unfortunate innocent to perfection, scoring off the fact that she was a girl. Carole Burnett and Betty Hutton had the same approach – win the audience over as a nice girl, then be the victim of circumstance.

Of course, in today's climate of political correctness this may seem by some people to be selling women short; however that ability to laugh at yourself, whether male or female, is one to which Australian audiences relate and comedians regularly employ in their routines. It helps the audience relax and enjoy the show.

Every professional knows that the audience must first of all like them, otherwise resentment replaces respect and the audience will never laugh. Being a likeable person can be cultivated like a facade, a veneer. But the comedian who is regarded as a mate, a friend, sharing fun happenings is, as they say, 'home and hosed'.

He said he liked taking home experienced girls. I said, 'I'm not an experienced girl.' He said, 'Ya not home yet.'

*A*n Australian and an Englishman were in a prisoner of war camp when they both got called out for punishment.

The commandant said: *You will both be beaten across your bare back with the steel whip. But because I am a merciful man, I will allow you to place something over your back to help protect you against the intense pain.*

The Pom stepped forward and said: *I don't want anything on my back. I'm British and I'm not afraid of you or your whip. The English are a race of brave heroes!*

So be it! said the commandant. Then, as he turned to the Aussie, he asked: *And what do you want on your back?*

The Aussie said: *The Pom!!*

A horse walked up to a bookie at Flemington and wanted to back himself. The bookmaker was astounded!

The horse said: *What's the matter, haven't you ever seen a talking horse before?*

That's not it, said the bookie, *I just can't believe you think you can win!*

A little bloke with a high-pitched voice and a lisp walked into a cafe and said to the waiter behind the counter: *I'll have a toathted thandwich, thankth.*

Thertainly Thir! said the waiter in the same high voice.

The little bloke was offended. *Hey, are you mocking me?* he asked.

No, no, said the waiter, *thith ith the way I talk!*

Well, alright then, said the little bloke.

Then another bloke, in a suit, walked into the cafe and said to the waiter: *I'll have a steak sandwich and a caesar salad.*

The waiter said: *Steak & salad, certainly Sir. Take a seat at table six and I'll serve you soon.*

The first little bloke was outraged! He called the waiter over and said: *I thought you thaid you weren't mocking me!*

The waiter said: *I wathn't mocking you, I wath mocking him!*

A yuppie crashed his BMW into a freight train. When the ambulance and police arrived he was in a terrible state.

Oh my God, he moaned.

Now stay calm, said the ambulance man.

Calm??!! Look at my BMW! It's ruined, said the yuppie.

But Sir, said the medico, *you're very badly injured. Your legs are all smashed up.*

Oh God, said the yuppie, *My Calvin Klein jeans! I just bought them. They're ruined!*

But Sir, said the ambulance man, *don't you feel pain? Your entire left arm is missing!*

Oh my God, said the yuppie, *where's my Rolex?!?!*

A bloke walked into a pub, and went up to the bar.

A beer for everyone in the pub, he said to the barman. *And one for yourself.*

Thanks mate, said the barman and proceeded to pour everybody a drink.

After the barman served everyone he came over to the bloke, finished his own beer, and said: *That's thirty-four dollars, mate.*

The bloke said: *I've got no money.*

The barman was furious. He grabbed the bloke, belted him in the mouth and threw him out on the street.

About an hour later the bloke was back. He walked up to the barman and said: *A beer for everyone in the pub, but nothing for you. You get dirty when you drink.*

A woman lost her house and car keys. She was very tired so she walked into a city park and went to sleep on a park bench. At about two o'clock in the morning she felt an arm around her and somebody kissing her neck. She jumped up. There was a drunk sitting on the bench beside her.

What do you think you're doing? she said. *I'm not some cheap pick-up!*

Oh yeah? he said. *Well what are you doing in my bed?*

*T*wo old army mates got together for a drink on Anzac Day. By closing time they were very drunk. They went back to the first one's house and had a few more beers. It was very late when the second bloke wondered what time it was, but he couldn't find a clock anywhere.

Hey Larry, he said. *You don't have a clock, mate. How do you tell the time?*

Larry said: *With my bugle.*

How can you tell the time with a bloody bugle? asked his mate.

I'll show ya, said Larry, and went to the window, opened it and blew his bugle loudly into the night.

Then a voice yelled out: *STOP that noise. Don't you know it's one-thirty in the bloody morning!*

A bloke was playing golf. As he walked down a fairway, he heard a voice.

Hey buddy, said the voice, which seemed to be coming from behind a bush. *Hey Buddy, have you got any toilet paper?*

No, said the bloke.

Hey buddy, said the voice. *Have you got any newspaper?*

No, I don't, said the bloke.

Hey buddy, said the voice, *have you got two fives for a ten?*

I told 'em me crook knee was knee-monia and me crook hip was only hip-notism.

I put 'arf a pound of sausages on a six to four favourite and we couldn't work it out in gravy.

He said, 'Walk this way.' I said, 'If I could walk that way, I wouldn't want the talcum powder.'

*D*uring the war two men were conscripted. They turned up for their medical check-up together. One went in to see the doctor while his mate waited outside for his turn.

Take off your clothes, said the doctor. The man stripped.

How long have you worn that truss? asked the doc.

About ten years, said the man.

Medically unfit, said the doctor, *you can go.*

You beauty, said the man. As soon as he got into the waiting room he said to his mate: *Quick, put this truss on. You won't have to go to the war.*

His mate grabbed the bloke's truss, dropped his pants, anxiously rushing to get the thing on.

Next, called the doctor from his office. *Strip,* said the doc.

Hmmm. How long have you worn that truss?

Twenty years, said the man.

Alright get dressed. I'm sending you to the Middle East! said the doctor.

The Middle East? cried the man. *But why?*

Mate, said the doctor, *anybody who can wear a truss inside out and upside down for twenty years can ride a bloody camel.*

A man and a woman were on safari up north when they came upon a giant crocodile sunning itself on the banks of the Burdekin River. They found themselves a ditch to hide in and got out their cameras.

After a while, they'd taken enough shots of the sleeping croc, so they tried to wake it up and get it to move. The bloke whistled, he yelled, he rustled some branches. But the croc didn't move an inch.

So the woman grabbed a stone and threw it at the beast, hitting it fair and square on the head. The crocodile roared, turned toward the man and woman and started charging at them. The woman grabbed her camera and started running for her life, but the bloke just stood there, laughing.

Run, you idiot! she screamed.

Why should I? he said. *You're the one who threw the stone!*

A blind man with a seeing-eye dog stood at a pedestrian crossing, waiting to cross the street. The light turned green and the dog didn't move. When the red light started flashing, the dog started to lead the man across. The lights changed and a truck nearly collected the blind man. When he got to the kerb he got out a dog biscuit for the dog.

A bloke who saw what happened came over and said: *That dog nearly got you killed! Why are you giving him a biscuit?*

The blind man said: *I'm trying to find out where his head is so I can kick him in the arse.*

*A*n Aussie had just finished wallpapering his house, when his English neighbour came in to visit.

This is a great wallpapering job, said the man. *Did you do it yourself?*

Sure did! said the Aussie.

You know something, said the Englishman, *you could help me out. You see, our houses are exactly the same size, and I was thinking of wallpapering myself. But the hardest part is working out how many rolls to buy. Tell me, when you did this place, how many rolls did you buy?*

I bought fourteen, said the Aussie.

Thanks very much, said the Pom, and left. He was back a week later. *Hey, I've got four rolls left over*, he said.

The Aussie said: *No kidding. Me too!*

A boy was climbing over a picket fence when he slipped; causing each leg to go either side of the fence, landing on the point of the paling right where it hurts. He ran to his doctor who was from India.

Doc, he said, *you gotta help me!*

The doctor enquired in a heavy Indian accent: *Well what is the matter with you, boy?*

The boy said: *I can't say, doc, just help me!*

What is the matter with you boy? insisted the doc.

Alright doc, said the boy. *It's my birdy! It's my birdy!*

The doctor said: *Well, many happy returns!*

*A*n Aussie explorer was shipwrecked on an island. As he crawled onto the beach, a bunch of ferocious head-hunters surrounded him.

I'm buggered, said the explorer.

No, you're not, boomed a voice from the sky.

The explorer said: *Is that you God?*

Yes, said God. *Now listen: you're not buggered yet. Here's what to do. These natives will take you to their Chief. When he approaches you, spit in his eye, and kick him in the jewels!*

If you say so God, said the explorer.

So he was dragged by the head-hunters through the jungle to their village. Out of a hut came the chief. He walked up to the Aussie, who then spat at him and kicked him right in the Jatz crackers. The Chief roared in rage. The tribesmen raised their spears and surrounded the Aussie.

God said: *Now you're buggered!*

*A*n Aussie was on holidays in America when he visited an Indian reservation. He saw a teepee beside the road with a sign outside: 'Chief Moosehead, He Knows All. He Remembers All!'

The Aussie decided to put the Indian to a test. He went inside the tent and said to the Chief: *What did I have for breakfast this morning?*

The Chief said: *Eggs!*

It was true, so the Aussie went on his way. About ten years later, he ran into the very same Indian Chief while the Chief was visiting Australia.

How! said the Aussie.

Scrambled, said the Chief.

A bloke from the bush got work in the city on a building site. He saw an ad in the paper offering a room and meals for $100 a week. So he turned up on the doorstep, rang the doorbell and a woman came to the door.

All meals? he asked.

Yes, she said.

So he moved in. The next morning he awoke to find his breakfast on the table and his lunch, a salad sandwich, wrapped in foil to take to work. When he got home that night, the woman said: *How was lunch?*

He said: *Lovely, but not enough.*

The next morning she'd made him three peanut butter sandwiches. Off he went to work. That night she asked him how lunch was today.

Lovely, he said, *but not enough.*

So the next morning she made him four vegemite sandwiches and eight cheese sandwiches.

Off he went, and that night the woman asked again: *How was lunch?*

Very nice, he said, *but still not enough.*

She thought: *Right, I'll fix this mongrel.* She went down to the supermarket and bought a French stick that was eight feet long if it was an inch, and into it she put a gallon of butter, three heads of lettuce, fourteen cans of beetroot, two pounds of ham, twelve tins of sardines, four jars of pickles, nine cucumbers, twenty-one tomatoes, sixteen slices of cheese, half a mullet and a parsnip!! She gave it to him the next morning wrapped in foil, and he went off to work. That night she asked him how it was.

Lovely, he said, *but I see you're back to one sandwich again!*

MAURIE'S WISDOM

Laughing at others' misfortune seems to be a universal recipe for humour and can be purely visual. Long before film and television presented spoken comedy, Charlie Chaplin's humour was largely at the expense of some unfortunate so-called villain, and often very cruel. His clever acrobatics were incorporated into many a combat which produced hysterical laughter from his audiences. They would have been lulled into accepting the downfall of his opponents because his clever plots usually began with him being kind to a blind flower girl, a crying baby or a poverty-stricken family, so that his subsequent exploits seemed heroic.

Buster Keaton, another very funny silent movie star, relied heavily on his exceptional talent for acrobatics – his fans and followers could always count on lots of prat-falls and falling about. This approach to getting laughs was so successful that many comedians over the years have incorporated it into their routines.

Knockabout comedians like Laurel and Hardy formed double acts, then trios such as the Ritz Brothers and the Marx Brothers arrived, all exploiting the physical aspects of this kind of slapstick humour.

This zany, pre-television era of comedy involved a fair amount of physical danger. The Three Stooges' playful approach to mishaps verged on violence. At that time slapstick comedy evolved to such an extent that silent movie casts expanded to include the combined talents of non-star comedians, stunt men and knockabout clowns. The world-famous Keystone Cops were one product of this trend.

Slapstick is still universally entertaining – people tripping, falling, or on the receiving end of something physically hurtful in 'Funniest Home Videos' programs are extremely popular. When it comes to jokes, we have all become used to finding humour in others' misfortune – it can be positively hilarious!

They made a mistake and put me among the lady dogs. Were you highly commended? No, but I was highly delighted.

A jockey was sitting on his horse in the mounting yard when the trainer approached and popped something in the horse's mouth.

What's that you're giving him? asked the jockey.

Just a peppermint, said the trainer.

Just then, the Chief Steward walked over. *I just saw you slip something into that horse's mouth,* he said. *What was it?*

It's a peppermint Sir, said the trainer. *Here, try one.* He handed the trainer one. *I'll have one myself, just to show you there's nothing funny going on.*

So the trainer and the Chief Steward popped the things in their mouths.

Alright, but you can't be too careful, said the Chief Steward, and walked off.

The trainer turned to the jockey and said: *Alright, now let the horse lead. Let him go in the straight. He'll be flying. In fact, if you hear anything passing you, it'll either be me, or the Chief Steward.*

I went into a fruit shop one day and all I could see was salt. The shelves were lined with boxes of salt. The floor was covered with bags of salt. Packets and packets of salt.

I said to the fruit shop owner: *You must sell a lot of salt. As a matter of fact, you must be the best salt salesman in the world.*

As a matter of fact, he said, *I don't sell much salt at all. But the guy who sells me salt – now there's a salt salesman!*

A toothbrush salesman consistently outsold his co-workers. The boss asked him what his secret was. Just how did he sell so many toothbrushes?

Well, said the salesman, *it's like this. I set up a table outside the city railway station. Then I put up a sign that says 'Free Pie Tasting' and I give pieces of pie to passers-by. The pies taste terrible. When they ask me what's in the pies, I tell them it's goat shit. Then I ask them if they want to buy a toothbrush.*

A bloke took his dog into a pub. He walked up to the barman and said: *If you give me a hundred bucks and free beer, I'll stay here with my talking dog.*

Talking dog is he? said the barman. *I don't believe it, make him talk.*

So the bloke turned to the dog and said: *Rover, what grows on trees?*

The dog said: *BARK.*

Nonsense, said the barman. *The dog's a fake.*

Alright, said the bloke. *I'll try another question. Rover, what's on top of a house?*

The dog said: *ROOF, ROOF.*

You're having a lend of me, said the barman, and threw the bloke and his dog out onto the street.

As they sat together in the gutter, the bloke said to the dog: *Well that was a pretty poor display, Rover.*

The dog said: *Well frankly Andrew, you were the one asking the questions.*

A bloke walked out of his house to find his neighbour piling rubbish up on the nature strip.

G'day, said the bloke, *I haven't seen you for a while.*

That's right, said the man, continuing to pile rubbish onto his nature strip.

Where's ya bin? said the bloke.

I bin in Queensland, said the man.

No, you don't understand. Where's ya wheelie bin? said the bloke.

Well, I wheelie been in jail, said the man, *but I'm telling everybody I bin in Queensland.*

A travel agent had just finished a very good week, when he noticed an old man and an old woman looking at the specials advertised on his window.

I've gone so well this week, he thought, *I'd like to do these old people a good turn.*

So he went out to the front of his shop and ushered them inside. *How would both of you like to go to Surfers Paradise for a week, all expenses paid?* he asked them.

I'd love to, said the old man.

How kind, said the old woman.

About ten days later the old man came to see the travel agent. *Thank you so much for the trip*, said the old bloke. *The flight was marvellous, the hotel was beautiful, and the scenery was gorgeous. Just one question.*

What's that? said the travel agent.

Who was that old woman staying with me?

A bloke stuck his head over the back fence to find his neighbour digging a huge hole in his backyard.

What're you doing? asked the bloke.

Burying my cat, replied the neighbour.

The bloke said: *That's a bloody big hole for a cat!*

The neighbour said: *Well, he's inside your German Shepherd!!*

A bloke walked into a pub on a Monday morning and ordered two beers. He took them over to a table, put one beer on one side of the table and one beer on the other side of the table. He went around to the first side, drank the first beer, then went around to the other side and drank the second beer, then left the pub. The barman watched all this with great curiosity.

The next Monday, the bloke was back, and ordered two beers, took them over to a table and went through the same routine. One on one side; one on the other; drank them separately; and got up to go.

Before he left, the barman, who again had been watching, called the bloke back. *Listen, mate*, he said, *I don't mean to bother you, but what's the story with the two beers?*

The bloke said: *It's like this, my mate's in the army and he's had to go over to Somalia for six months and he asked me to have a beer for him every week 'til he gets back.*

Oh, I see, said the barman. *No worries.*

For the next month or so, the bloke came in every Monday and did the two beers routine. Then one week, he came in and ordered just one beer. He took it over to a table and put it down; then went over to the other side and sat there for a minute; then got up, went around and drank the beer and started to leave.

The barman, watching, called after him: *Hey, mate, what's happened?* he said. *You only bought one beer. Is your friend alright?*

Oh yeah, said the bloke. *He's fine. It's just that I've decided to give up the grog.*

A copper pulled over a motorist on the freeway.

Get out of the car please Sir, said the cop, *and step to the rear of the vehicle.*

The driver got out of the car and followed the cop around to the back of the car.

Sir, said the copper, *your rear tail light is out.*

Oh my God, screamed the driver. *Oh no, this is terrible. Oh Lord, I don't believe it. What am I going to do?* Then he threw himself on the ground.

Settle down Sir, said the cop, *it's only a tail light!*

Bugger the tail light, said the driver, *where's the bloody caravan?*

A woman was testifying in the Family Court.

Your Honour, she said, *I want a divorce. My husband beats me up every night.*

Her husband stood up and said: *Don't listen to her, your Honour, she's punch-drunk.*

MAURIE'S WISDOM

Many children learning musical instruments would probably never have predicted that their serious years of study and dedication could eventually be presented as comedy, and even relied on by world-famous comedians.

When the world wasn't in such a hurry, before the electronic media played such a large part in our lives, people in general were more inclined to appreciate the advantages of entertaining by playing a musical instrument. Celebrated comedy stars used their serious musical abilities to great advantage. The famous Jack Benny, when doing a stage performance, relied heavily on his ability to play the violin. He used his own pre-recorded voice while he played the violin very seriously – the laughs came thick and fast as the audience heard his private thoughts.

Another versatile American funny man, well known to Australians who remember the vaudeville era, was Will Mahoney. His clever knockabout ability was used to the hilt in sketches like 'The Ice Man Cometh', in which he slid all over the stage on blocks of ice; and his boxing sketch, in which his small frame dodged and weaved around a huge opponent like an infuriating mosquito. The highlight of all his performances, however, involved the playing of a very large xylophone – but not in any ordinary way. Will danced with the musical hammers attached to the front of his shoes and made fantastic music by dancing on top of the instrument.

English comedians were often also talented musicians. George Formby, for example, was renowned for his banjo playing, Dudley Moore is a great piano player and Reg Varney featured music in his stage act, particularly the playing of the piano-accordion. Victor Borge, from Denmark, remained an international favourite by centring almost all of his wonderful comedy routines around a legitimate activity that was no doubt his original goal in life: to be a great concert pianist. Of course, he was hailed as the world's funniest piano player!

If that's the place where bees get honey: funny no more honey from the bee: I'll stick to treacle, no more honey from the bee.

*A*n Aussie soldier during the war was having a drink in a bar in Singapore, when a big Yank came up behind him and went: *HII YAH, WHACK!* Down went the Aussie.

The Yank said: *Hey Aussie, that was judo from Japan.*

The Aussie got up, brushed himself down, and went back to his beer. The Yank came up behind him again and went: *EEEE-HAAA YIP, WHACK!* Down went the Aussie again.

The Yank bloke said: *Hey, Aussie, that was karate from Korea.*

The Aussie got up and left the bar. He was back in ten minutes, walked up behind the Yank and went: *HEEE YAH, WHACK!* Down went the Yank, out cold.

The Aussie said: *When that Yank mongrel comes to, tell him that was a crowbar from K-Mart!*

A man was sitting in his seat at the AFL Grand Final at the MCG. The match was a sellout, but the seat beside him was empty. The game was about to start and the seat was still empty, so he leaned over to the bloke on the other side of the empty seat and said: *Somebody's running late.*

The bloke said: *Actually, that's my wife's seat and she won't be coming.*

Why not? asked the first man.

Unfortunately, after I bought the tickets, she died, said the bloke.

That's terrible, said the first man. *Listen, I don't mean to sound heartless, but couldn't you have given the seat to one of your friends?*

I couldn't, said the bloke. *They're all at the funeral!*

A group of Irish blokes loyal to the IRA was planning a murder/kidnapping of Britain's Prime Minister, Tony Blair. Clustered together under London Bridge, the blokes were going over the plan.

Alright, said Paddy, *one last time. Tony Blair will leave his office at 4.20 p.m. At 4.25 p.m. he'll pass Trafalgar Square. At 4.32 p.m. he'll enter the approach to this bridge above us here. At 4.34 p.m. his car will be directly overhead, at which time we detonate the bomb in the bridge, stopping his car. We then storm the vehicle, kill the driver and bodyguards, grab the Prime Minister, knock him out, and put him in our van. At 4.51 p.m. we arrive at our hideout where we make the ransom call. And at 4.57 p.m. we murder the Prime Minister.*

Alright, let's check our watches . . . hang on, it's 5.22 p.m. They're late!! Gee, I hope they're alright.

*T*wo packets of potato chips walked into a bar. One of the packets of potato chips walked up to the barman and said: *Two beers mate.*

The barman said: *Sorry buddy, but we don't serve food here.*

*A*l Capone, the Mafia gangster, was approached by his six-year-old son.

Poppa, said the kid, *I want a bike.*

Well, said Capone, *if you want a bike, pray to the Baby Jesus before you go to sleep tonight, and maybe he'll send you a bike.*

So that night, the kid got down on his knees beside his bed and said: *Please Lord Jesus, please give me a bike. Amen.* Then he got into bed and went to sleep.

In the morning there was no bike, so the next night he got down on his knees again and prayed: *Please Lord Jesus. Maybe you didn't hear me last night. Please, oh please give me a bike.* Then he got into bed and waited.

At about 3.00 a.m. there was still no bike, so the kid got up, turned the light on, went over to his dresser, got the statue of Mary, the Madonna, and took it back to his bed and put it under his pillow.

The next morning he got out of bed and got down on his knees to pray: *Dear Baby Jesus*, he said. *You get me the bike and you get your mother back!*

*A*n old bloke was on his deathbed. His missus and family were gathered around him.

Norm, his wife said, you've been a good husband to me for forty years. You haven't got long, Norm. Is there anything you want, love?

The old bloke lifted his head and said: *Well actually, Vera, I'd love a glass of beer from that jug over there.*

She said: *Well you can't! That's for the wake!*

*A*n elderly couple were discussing their love-life in a doctor's surgery. They asked the doctor to observe their lovemaking and advise them on how they could improve the situation.

The doctor was reluctant but decided to be kind. He observed the lovemaking and advised the elderly couple as requested.

I can't see a medical reason for any problem with your love-life, he said.

The old couple thanked the doctor and left the surgery.

Next week they were back again with the same request, and the doctor once again advised them that there was nothing wrong with their lovemaking. Everything was perfectly normal.

When the couple returned a third time the doctor decided to reject them as patients.

Please don't turn us away, they pleaded.

You see, said the man, *we can't go to her place, she's married; we can't go to my place, I'm married; a hotel costs one hundred dollars a night; a motel costs eighty dollars a night. You only charge thirty dollars and we can get half of that back on Medicare!*

A telephone saleswoman rang a random number out of the telephone book, trying to sell encyclopedias. A little girl answered the 'phone in a whisper.

Hello, said the saleswoman.

Hello, whispered the child.

Is mummy there? asked the woman.

Yes, but she's busy, said the little girl.

The saleswoman said: *Well, is your daddy there?*

Yes, whispered the child, *but he's busy too.*

Well, is anyone else there? asked the woman.

Yes, a fireman, said the girl.

A fireman? said the woman. *Well can I speak to him, then?*

No, whispered the kid, *he's busy too.*

The woman said: *Is anybody else there?*

Yes, whispered the little girl. *A policeman.*

A policeman? said the woman. *Can I speak to him?*

The little girl said: *No, he's busy as well.*

The woman said: *Well what are they all busy doing?*

The little girl whispered: *Looking for me.*

A fella walks into a bar next to a hospital and says to the barman: *I'll have a double scotch, mate, but I shouldn't be having it with what I've got.*

The barman gave him the drink.

The bloke said: *And give me a double martini, but I shouldn't be having it with what I've got.*

The barman gave him the martini.

And you'd better give me a boilermaker, with a beer chaser, said the bloke, *but I really shouldn't be having any of this with what I've got.*

The barman gave him the drinks and said: *I don't like to be nosey, mate, but what HAVE you got?*

The bloke said: *Forty cents.*

A woman took her son to the doctor because he was tired all the time and kept catching colds. The doctor asked about the child's diet.

All he eats is snooker balls, said Mum.

The doctor was amazed. *Snooker balls?* he asked.

Yes that's right, she said, *for breakfast, he'll have three reds and a brown. For lunch he'll have four reds, a pink, a yellow and a blue. And for dinner, he'll have the black, and five or six reds.*

Well there's your trouble, said the doctor. *Not enough greens.*

I'll have you know I'm king in our house. Yes Dad, I know. I was there the night mum crowned ya!

Somewhere overweight people just like me must have somewhere where they don't count every calorie.

Val always said that I was warm in winter and shady in the summer.

A vacuum cleaner salesman knocked on the door of a farmhouse. A woman came to the door.

Madam, said the salesman, *I represent the Nifty Shifty Vacuum Company and Madam, we guarantee our vacuums are the best on the market. As a matter of fact,* he said, pushing his way inside the house, *I'm going to put some dirt and rubbish on your carpet and I will personally eat anything this cleaner doesn't pick up.*

But . . . said the woman.

No buts, Madam, said the salesman, *just watch and be amazed.*

So he poured a packet of sawdust on the carpet, then some iron filings, then a box of thumb tacks . . .

But . . . said the woman.

No buts, Madam, he said, *just watch and be amazed.*

On top of the other stuff, he poured some ice cream and then a round piece of dog poo into it all. *Now, Madam, don't be alarmed. I will personally eat every bit of that mess that the Nifty Shifty Vacuum cleaner doesn't pick up!*

She said: *Well would you like some pepper and salt,* she said, *because we haven't got the power on, yet!*

*T*hree drunks came staggering onto the platform at Central Station just as the train to Brisbane was pulling out.

Oh no, they yelled, *we've missed the train.*

The train driver saw the three on the platform and quickly radioed the guard at the rear. *There're three blokes on the platform. See if you can drag them on board as you pass them.*

Righto, said the guard.

As he approached the trio, the guard reached out and managed to grab two of them and heaved them onto the train, leaving one bloke swaying on the platform.

The guard yelled out at him: *Sorry, I couldn't get all three of you on board.*

That's alright, said the drunk, *but I think you got the two that came to see me off!*

*A*n Irishman and his brother were hauling a load of potatoes in a semitrailer when they came to a low bridge.

The sign on the bridge said: WARNING, LOW CLEARANCE: 3.9 METRES

Paddy said to Mick: *What's our height?*

Mick said: *4.2 metres.*

Paddy said: *There's no coppers around, I say we go under it anyway.*

*T*wo jackeroos were repairing fences in the outback when one of them sat down on a rock for a rest. As he sat, he disturbed a deadly brown snake which bit him on the bum.

Quick! He yelled to his mate. *A snake just bit me on the bum – go get help!*

So the second jackeroo jumped on his horse, rode to the nearest station and got on the radio to the Flying Doctors.

My mate's been bitten by a brown snake, he said.

The doctor said: *You'll have to suck the poison out, or he's going to die.*

So the jackeroo rode back out to his mate.

What did they say? asked his mate.

They said you're going to die, said the bloke.

A yuppie walked into a cafe to have a Corona with his real estate agent.

His estate agent said: *The drinks are on me. I just sold a house in Ballarat.*

Ballarat? said the yuppie. *The only good things to come out of Ballarat are football players and prostitutes!*

A huge bloke with tattoos all over him was standing behind the yuppie. He spun the yuppie 'round and said: *My wife comes from Ballarat!*

The yuppie said timidly: *Oh, really? What team does she play for?*

A bloke sat down at a stranger's table in a pub and said: *Mind if I join you?*

Not at all, said the seated man, *pull up a chair*.

Soon they were drinking and chatting like old mates. By about eleven o'clock that night, they were both very drunk.

The first bloke said: *Well, I'd better be on my way*.

Me too, said the second and stood up, but as soon as he did, he fell over.

Looks like you've had a bit too much to drink, said the first, *I'll help you home*.

So he picked him up and half-carried him to the door of the pub. While he opened the door, he leant the bloke against the wall, but he fell over again.

Gawd, said the bloke, *you ARE in a bad way*. So he lifted him out the door, somehow found out where the bloke lived, dragged him to his car and leant him against the bonnet while he opened the door. The bloke fell over again. He picked him up, bundled him into the passenger seat, got in the car, and drove to the bloke's home. When they got there, he got out and pulled the bloke out of the car. While he opened the front gate to the bloke's house, down he went again, smashing his face on the footpath.

Geez, he said, *I can't show up with you looking like this. Your missus will think I've been punching you up!*

So he took him to the front door, leant him against it, rang the doorbell, and ran away. When the bloke's wife opened the front door, he fell face first into the front hall.

Well that's lovely, she said. *Drunk! And you've forgotten your wheelchair again!*

A little girl asked her dad: *Daddy, what's thunder?*

I dunno, said her father.

She said: *Daddy, where does lightning come from?*

He replied: *I dunno.*

She asked: *Daddy, where does rain go?*

I dunno, said her father.

Daddy, she asked, *do you mind me asking you so many questions?*

Of course not, darling, he said. *How else are you going to learn anything?*

*T*wo Irish blokes walked into a pub in Adelaide. They walked up to the barman – a huge red-headed fellow – and asked in their best Irish accents for two pints of Guinness.

You're not Irish, are you? asked the barman.

Yes, we are, as a matter of fact, said the blokes.

Ooh, that's wonderful, to be sure, said the big barman. *I'm from Ireland myself, and I just love meeting up with my fellow countrymen. Tell me boys, what are your names?*

I'm Pat, said the first.

The barman said: *What do you mean 'Pat' . . . your name's Patrick. Patrick. Don't ever shorten such a wonderful Irish name. It's Patrick. You hear me? Patrick.* And he punched the bloke in the face, and then smashed a bottle over his head, saying: *That's Patrick!*

He turned to the second Irishman. *And what's your name?* he said.

The second bloke looked at his mate and said nervously, *Mick . . . Rick.*

MAURIE'S WISDOM

Many influences have undoubtedly made their mark on Australian performers. The evolution of the true-blue Aussie comedian, however, occurred in isolation from the rest of the world – before the jet age and modern communications made everything so much more accessible.

Australian comedians are respected and acknowledged throughout the world. As Australians, we recognise our own talented performers as being as good as, if not better, than the imported equivalent.

The development of Maurie Fields' talent had much to do with his upbringing. He had free tap dancing lessons as a child – his mother Eileen played piano for the local school and he tagged along when she played at dancing classes. Maurie had a natural singing voice, with a range that was comfortable in any key, and a perfect ear for harmony. He could play a variety of musical instruments including the banjo and ukelele, which he learned by attending his older sister's lessons.

As a school sports champion, Maurie was agile. He was a great dramatic actor, with a sense of timing that is usually inbuilt and can't be learned. No doubt, all of these attributes were enhanced by observing others, even if only subconsciously. He loved it all!

This superb joke teller known to all as 'That Great Aussie Bloke' became an icon, much loved by those of all ages, all professions and all denominations. He evolved into a man of exceptional persona by adapting all his observations. If he did have an ambition, it was the same desire that remained with him all his days: to make people laugh. Maurie Fields was happiest when he was doing just that.

Did you hear about the constipated accountant? He worked it out with a pencil.

A bride and groom dressed in their wedding clothes were in a hotel elevator, on their way to the honeymoon suite when a woman entered the lift. She pressed for her floor, then turned to the groom and said: *Hello Barry. Why haven't you called me? I love you.*

The groom said: *Hello Rachel.* Then the woman got off at her floor.

The bride was furious. She hissed at the groom, *Who was that??!!*

Don't you start, he said, *I'm gonna have a hard enough time explaining YOU to HER!!*

A country cricket team was playing a neighbouring town. The bowler was getting ready to start his spell when he noticed that the umpire (provided by the opposition) was his father-in-law who hated him.

Oh well, he thought, *I'm sure he won't let his feelings get in the way of the game.*

So he bowled his first ball, which was nicked by the batsman to first slip.

Howzat? he shouted.

Not out, said the umpire.

So the bowler went back and bowled a lovely delivery, catching the batsman plumb LBW.

Howzat? he roared at the umpire.

Not out, said the umpire.

I'll fix this guy, said the bowler.

He started his run up at the fence, and let fly an enormous full toss. It went straight through the batsman's legs and hit the middle stump, breaking it in half. He turned to his father-in-law, the umpire and said: *Geez, Bert, I nearly bloody got him, that time!*

*I*n a state of agitation, a vicar rang the police.

Someone's stolen my bike, he said.

The copper said: *Well, you can bet it's one of your parishioners, so I'll tell you what to do. Next Sunday, during your sermon, do a big special on the Ten Commandments. When you get to the Seventh Commandment: 'Thou shalt not steal', have a look at your congregation. The one who stole your bike will be looking very guilty.*

Alright then, said the Vicar, *I'll try it.*

About a week later the copper saw the Vicar riding down the street on his pushbike.

Hey Father, he called. *I see you've got your bike back. Did you follow my advice?*

I certainly did, said the Vicar. *I gave a sermon on the Ten Commandments, but when I got to the Fourth Commandment: 'Thou shalt not commit adultery', I remembered where I'd left my bike!*

*A*n Australian, an American and an Irishman were captured by South American Contra rebels and were sentenced to die by firing squad.

The Australian was first up. He stood in front of the firing squad and the captain said: *Ready, aim* . . .

The Aussie yelled out: *EARTHQUAKE!!*

The soldiers dropped their guns and looked around in a panic. During the confusion, the Aussie made his escape.

The captain got them back in line and stood the American in front of them. He said: *Squad, ready, aim* . . .

And the American shouted: *FLOOD!!*

Again they turned around and he also made his escape.

Once more, the captain got them in line and stood the Irishman in front of them. *Squad, ready, aim* . . .

And the Irishman shouted: *FIRE!!*

A bloke, his missus and his mother-in-law were driving down the freeway, when a copper pulled them over.

What've I done? asked the bloke.

Nothing at all, Sir, said the copper. *You were the one millionth car to use that overpass back there and the government has given you a cheque for ten thousand dollars! What do you think you'll do with the money?*

Gee, said the bloke, *I might invest in some driving lessons and finally get myself a licence!*

What??!! said the copper.

The bloke's wife leant over and said: *Oh don't listen to him Officer, he's drunk.*

Drunk?? said the copper. *That's it, get out of the car.*

Just then his old mother-in-law stuck her head over from the back seat and said: *You see, I told you there'd be nothing but trouble driving a stolen vehicle!*

A solicitor opened an office in Melbourne. It had a great view in a prestigious building. He hired a secretary and some office furniture.

At 9.00 a.m. on his first morning, he sat at his desk and started sharpening his pencils. At 11.15 a.m. his secretary knocked at his door, saying a man was here to see him.

Fabulous, he thought, *my first client. I really must make a good impression.*

So he told his secretary to send in the bloke. He picked up his phone and as the man walked in, he said: *No, I won't accept a million for my client. I want three million and not a penny less!* and slammed the receiver down.

He looked up at the man and said: *Now, what can I do for you Sir?*

The bloke said: *I'm from Telstra. I've come to connect the phone.*

*W*ay back early this century, an African American arrived at the Pearly Gates.

I wanna come into heaven, he said.

Now, St Peter was a good ol' Southern boy at heart and wasn't sure if he should let a negro into heaven with the white folk, so he said: *Well, boy, you have to have done something very brave during your life to get into heaven.*

I did! I did! said the black guy. *I married a white girl in a white church in Alabama surrounded by two hundred members of the Klu Klux Klan!*

St Peter said: *My Lord, that was brave. When did you do that?*

The black guy said: *About three minutes ago.*

A market research company was employed by a plumbing group to find out which way people faced in the bath – with their feet toward the taps, or their back toward the taps. They interviewed 2000 people, and 1999 people said they sat with their feet toward the taps, and only one person sat with their back toward the taps.

The plumbing company were amazed at the result and rang the odd man out.

Sir, they said, *may we ask why, out of 2000 people, you are the only one who sits with their back toward the taps?*

The bloke replied: *Because I don't have a bath plug.*

*D*uring the Vietnam war, an Australian General was inspecting the wounded in an army hospital in South Vietnam, when he came upon a particularly badly injured Aussie soldier.

Good Lord, man, said the General, *what happened to you out there?*

The soldier said: *Well, it's like this Sir. They all look alike to me in the jungle. I can't tell the North Vietnamese from the South Vietnamese. It's getting me in a lot of trouble.*

The General gave the man some advice. *This is what you do*, he said. *If you're creeping through the jungle and you hear a noise, yell out 'HO CHI MIN'S A MONGREL!' and if the bloke sticks his head up and argues, BANG! You've got him!*

Alright Sir, said the soldier, *I'll try it.*

About six weeks later, the same General was inspecting a hospital, and there was the same soldier in a very bad way – he was covered in bandages, missing an arm, broken legs, terrible.

My God, said the General. *What happened out there man? Didn't you follow my advice?*

The soldier said: *Sure did Sir. I was creeping through the jungle and I heard a noise, so I yelled out: 'HO CHI MIN'S A MONGREL', and he yelled out, 'SO'S HAROLD HOLT,' and while we were shaking hands, a tank ran over the both of us!!*

A bloke went to the psychiatrist about his wife.

Doc, it's amazing, he said, *she thinks she's a horse!*

The shrink said: *What do you mean, she thinks she's a horse?*

She really does, doc, said the bloke. *She sleeps standing up. All she eats is hay. She's growing hair down the back of her neck. She whinnies.*

The psychiatrist said: *This sounds extremely serious. Now I should warn you, treatment for this sort of condition can take a long time, and it could be very expensive.*

That's alright, said the bloke. *Money's no object. She's won her last three starts.*

A little girl was drawing with crayons, sitting at the kitchen table. Her mother walked in and asked: *What are you drawing, Sharon?*

She said: *A picture of God.*

Her mother said: *Don't be silly, nobody knows what God looks like!*

The little girl said: *Well, they will when I'm finished.*

A woman got a job as a kindergarten teacher. On her first day she decided to get to know her young pupils. She spotted a pretty little girl in the front row.

What's your name? asked the teacher.

Jasmine, said the little girl.

And why are you called Jasmine? asked the teacher.

Well, said the girl, *when Mummy had me in her tummy, she sat in our garden and a jasmine leaf fell on her tummy, so she called me Jasmine.*

That's lovely, said the teacher. Turning to another pretty girl in a pink dress, she said: *And what's your name?*

The little girl said: *My name's Blossom.*

And why are you called Blossom? asked the teacher.

Well, when I was in Mummy's tummy, said the girl, *she was lying in our backyard under a tree, and a blossom fell on her tummy, so she called me Blossom.*

I see said the teacher. Then she spotted an ugly, ugly, cross-eyed boy with buck teeth, one ear, and a bent nose, sitting at the back.

And you up the back, she said to him, *what's your name?*

The boy said: *Bluestone.*

A man and his wife were on their honeymoon. The bloke was a mad keen golfer, so on the first day of their honeymoon, he wanted to go and play golf at the local country course.

Well, said his new bride, *I'll come and caddy for you.*

So off they went. Everything was going fine until the 14th hole, a par three, where he hit off and went away to the right, landing in an old barn. When they found the ball, which had landed inside the barn, the bloke was furious, because he'd have to take a drop and the penalty was going to ruin his score.

Wait, said his wife. *If I hold the barn door open, you can see the green. Hit it past me, through the door and you could save the hole.*

So the bloke gave it a try, but instead of hitting through the open door, he hit his wife in the head, killing her stone-dead.

About ten years later, the man had remarried and was on holiday with his second wife at the same country golf course. As luck would have it, he pushed the ball right on the 14th and landed inside the barn again.

Don't worry, said his new bride. *If I hold this door open, you can hit the green from here.*

Don't be insane, said the bloke. *Last time I tried that I scored a triple bogey!*

A bloke was in a doctor's surgery waiting for the results of his medical check-up.

The doctor said: *Well, I've got good news and I've got bad news.*

The patient said: *What's the bad news?*

You've got cancer, said the doctor.

The patient asked: *What's the good news?*

The doctor said: *I'm sleeping with my cute, red-headed nurse.*

*A*n Aussie and a Yank were chatting in a country pub.

I've got two hundred acres up the road, said the Aussie. *Keeps me busy.*

Two hundred acres??!! said the Yank. *Why, I've got a ranch in Texas that's so big, I can ride my horse from the east boundary, ride all day, and still not reach the west boundary! What do you think of that?*

Yeah, laughed the Aussie, *I used to have a clapped-out old horse like that myself.*

*T*he Victorian Railways were running an efficiency test for their country level crossing signal operators. The Inspector sat in his office with a bloke who worked at the Sunraysia Highway Crossing, near Mildura.

Alright, said the Inspector, *here's the situation. Imagine a freight train is approaching the level crossing, and a semitrailer is stuck across the crossing. What do you do?*

The bloke said: *I'd help the driver move the semitrailer.*

You can't, said the Inspector, *he's unconscious in the bushes.*

Then I'd move it myself, said the bloke.

You can't, said the Inspector, *it's broken down.*

Then, said the bloke, *I'd radio the train to stop.*

You can't, the radio's dead, the Inspector said.

The bloke said: *Then I'd turn the signals for the train to red.*

You can't, said the Inspector, *they're not working.*

Then I'd get out a red flag and signal the driver, said the bloke.

You can't, it's night, said the Inspector.

Well then I'd go wake up the wife, said the bloke.

Why? asked the Inspector. *What could she do?*

Nothing, replied the bloke, *but she's never seen a big train crash before!*

INDEX

Abbott and Costello, 68
acrobatics, 100
adultery, 38
AFL Grand Final, 115
Allen, Gracie, 68
American, 18, 37, 61, 139
   African, 142
army, 30, 76, 88, 144
Australian, 18, 61, 82, 95,
   97, 98, 139, 150
   accent, 32
   jokes, 8, 32

Ball, Lucille, 80
bank, 11
bar, 114, 117, 122
bath, 143
battery, 35
Benny, Jack, 112
blind man, 25, 94
Borge, Victor, 112
bride and groom, 136
buffalo, 40
burlesque, 44
Burnett, Carole, 80
Burns, George, 68

cafe, 84, 130
canary, 46
Capone, Al, 118
cat, 108
Chaplin, Charlie, 100
comediennes, 80
commandments, 16, 138
Cook, Peter, 68
cowboy, 39, 66
crabs, 41
cricket, 70, 137
crocodile, 93

Daley, Cass, 80
Diller, Phyllis, 80
doctor, 7, 10, 22, 34, 79,
   92, 96, 120, 123, 145,
   149
dog, 18, 24, 36, 62, 94,
   105, 108
drunk, 12, 43, 55, 87,
   127

Englishman, 35, 82, 95

Family Court, 111
family, 27, 119
farm, 13, 64

Formby, George, 112
fruit shop, 103
girl, little, 24, 121, 132, 146
golf, 23, 52, 58, 67, 78,
   89, 148
grandchildren, 22
Greenwood, Charlotte, 80
greyhound, 47

Hale and Pace, 68
head-hunters, 97
hearing aid, 14
heaven, 142
hitchhiker, 73
Holt, Harold, 144
horse, 59, 102
horseracing, 102
hospital, 29, 122
Hutton, Betty, 80

Indian reservation, 98
Irish, 17, 36, 65, 76, 116,
   128, 133, 139
Italian, 63

jackeroos, 129
Jewish, 15, 27, 60
joke telling, 8
   partnerships in, 68
jumbo jet, 41

Keaton, Buster, 100
Kentucky Derby, 37
Keystone cops, 100

Laurel and Hardy, 100
Logie Award, 6
lucky charms, 31

Mahoney, Will, 112
market research, 143
Martin and Lewis, 68
Marx Brothers, the, 100
Maurie's Wisdom, 8, 32,
   44, 68, 80, 100, 112,
   134
monkeys, 19
Moore, Dudley, 68, 112
Morecombe and Wise, 68
Moses, 16
mother-in-law, 74, 140
musical instruments, 112,
   134

Nevada Desert, 61
nightclub, 72
O'Brien, Virginia, 80
obituaries, 15
old bloke, 34, 71, 119

paint, 50
pig, three-legged, 13
police, 26, 40, 43, 49, 77,
   110, 138, 140
political correctness, 80
politics, 64
porch, 50
potato chips, 117
prison, 54
prisoner of war, 82
psychiatrist, 145
pub, 23, 31, 42, 55, 65, 86,
   105, 109, 131, 133, 150

racehorse, 37, 47, 83
Raye, Martha, 80
restaurant, 28
revue, 44
rhyming slang, 32
Ritz Brothers, the, 100

salesman, 103, 104, 126
saleswoman, 121
sandwiches, 99
school friends, 31
shark, 48
silent movies, 44, 100
slapstick, 44, 100
snake, 53, 129
solicitor, 141
squid, 48
steer, 12
supernatural, 75

teacher, 51, 62, 147
Telstra, 141
Three Stooges, the, 100
train, 26, 85, 127, 151
travel agent, 107
traveller's cheques, 19
Tullamarine airport, 35
Two Ronnies, the, 68

ukulele, 56, 134

variety, 44, 68
Varney, Reg, 112
vaudeville, 44, 68
vet, 46
vicar, 138
Volvo, 15

wallpapering, 95
waiter, 84
war, 82, 92, 114, 144

wheelie bin, 106

yuppie, 85, 130